I Am William

I Am William

Text
Rébecca Déraspe

Translation by
Leanna Brodie

Music
Chloé Lacasse
Benoit Landry

I Am William
first published 2022 by Scirocco Drama
An imprint of J. Gordon Shillingford Publishing Inc.
© 2022 Leanna Brodie

Scirocco Drama Editor: Glenda MacFarlane
Cover design by Doowah Design
Photo of Rébecca Déraspe by Lucas Harrison Rupnik
Photo of Leanna Brodie by Kristine Cofsky
Stratford Festival production photos by David Hou
Théâtre Le Clou production photos by François Godard

Printed and bound in Canada on 100% post-consumer recycled paper.
We acknowledge the financial support of the Manitoba Arts Council and
The Canada Council for the Arts for our publishing program.

Production inquiries to:
Michael Petrasek
Kensington Literary Representation
34 St. Andrew Street
Toronto, ON
M5T 1K6
416.848.9648
kensingtonlit@rogers.com

Library and Archives Canada Cataloguing in Publication

Title: I am William / Rébecca Déraspe ; translated by Leanna Brodie.
Other titles: Je suis William. English
Names: Déraspe, Rébecca, 1983- author. | Brodie, Leanna, translator.
Description: Translation of: Je suis William. | A play.
Identifiers: Canadiana (print) 2022019632X | Canadiana (ebook) 20220196427 |
ISBN 9781927922958 (softcover) | ISBN 9781990737114 (HTML)

Classification: LCC PS8607.E715 J413 2022 | DDC C842/.6—dc23

J. Gordon Shillingford Publishing
P.O. Box 86, RPO Corydon Avenue, Winnipeg, MB Canada R3M 3S3

Rébecca Déraspe, Playwright

Rébecca Déraspe graduated from the playwriting programme of the National Theatre School of Canada in May 2010. She is the author of a number of internationally produced and translated plays, including *Deux ans de votre vie (You Are Happy)*, *Plus que toi*, *Peau d'ours*, *Gamètes (Gametes)*, *Nino*, *Je suis William (I Am William)*, *Le merveilleux voyage de Réal de Montréal*, *Partout ailleurs*, *Nos petits doigts*, *Faire la leçon (The Lessons)*, and *Ceux qui se sont évaporés*. She has adapted several classics, including Shakespeare's *Romeo and Juliet* and *Twelfth Night* and Ibsen's *A Doll's House*. Her plays *Les filles du Saint-Laurent*, *Fanny*, and *Faire crier les murs* were recently produced in France and Québec, and she is now developing her play *Les glaces* at Théâtre la Licorne, where she has been a playwright-in-residence since 2018. Déraspe won the Prix Michel-Tremblay and the 2020 Montréal Critics' Prize for Best New Play for *Ceux qui se sont évaporés*; the 2018 Montréal Critic's Prize for Best Play for Young Audiences and the Prix Louise-Lahaye for *Je suis William*; the 2017 Montréal Critics' Prize for Best New Play for *Gamètes*, which toured throughout Québec and across Canada; and the 2010 BMO Financial Group Playwright's Prize for *Deux ans de votre vie*. She writes and hosts the web series *Le lexique de la polémique* for Savoir Média.

Leanna Brodie, Translator

Leanna Brodie's plays and libretti have been performed from Halifax to Vancouver, London to Auckland. *The Vic, For Home and Country, The Book of Esther*, and *Schoolhouse* are published by Talonbooks. She is also a noted translator of Québécois and Franco-Canadian drama whose recent productions include Hélène Ducharme's internationally acclaimed *Baobab*; David Paquet's award-winning *The Shoe* (The Cherry Artspace, Ithaca NY) and *Wildfire* (Upstream Theater, St. Louis MO and Factory Theatre, Toronto ON); Joe Jack et John's *Violette* (Espace Libre, Montréal PQ); Catherine Léger's *I Lost My Husband!* (Ruby Slippers Theatre/Gateway Theatre, Vancouver BC and Persephone Theatre, Saskatoon SK); Mohsen El Gharbi's *Omi Mouna* (Impact Festival, Kitchener ON and Infinithéâtre, Montréal QC) and Rébecca Déraspe's *You Are Happy* (GCTC and Red Theater Chicago). Three of her translations have been nominated for Tom Hendry Awards. She is currently translating new works by Fanny Britt, Rébecca Déraspe, Sébastien Harrisson, and Olivier Sylvestre; completing her MFA at the University of Calgary; teaching playwriting at UBC; and co-writing *Salesman in China* (a commission from the Stratford Festival) with Jovanni Sy.

www.leannabrodie.com

Playwright's Notes

When I was in school, I never noticed the inequalities that still remain between men and women. That battle, I thought, had been won a long time ago. I thought that I was free to pursue my dreams: that no one would prevent me from doing whatever I wanted, just because I was a girl. Then came the shock of reality. I hadn't gotten it completely wrong: it was true that no one was going to stop me from making my own decisions. I realized, however, that hundreds of years of inequities between men and women have had an effect on the basic structures of our world. We still carry baggage that subtly influences our perception of things. The glass ceiling; violence against women; the role of the mother within the home... all of them feed the imbalance between genders.

I wish that, as a child, I had learned about the lives of great women who made history. Because of course there were women authors, scientists, painters, composers, and philosophers well before the middle of the 19th century. Yet "Young Me" had no way of knowing that they had existed; had shaped the world, each in her own way; but had then been forgotten, hidden away, tossed into the garbage can of our past. When it comes to recording significant events, "The Timeline of History" can be an unreliable narrator. Nowadays, more and more books are being written to try to redress this erasure by honouring the achievements of female pioneers. I am proud that I can share them with my nine-year-old daughter, showing her examples of remarkable women blazing new trails.

I truly believe that I *Am William* is for everyone; however, I wrote this play for young people. For their intense need to find their place in the world. For their dreams. For the great and beautiful strength with which they envision the future. I thought about them. Every day. I thought of their struggles. Their desires. Their battles. I thought of their insatiable need to wrestle meaning out of the ordinary ups and downs of life. I thought of young people because I, for one, still feel very close to these passions, this heartbreak. And I wanted all of us together to tell this story of history, where reality and fiction speak to us of the Present.

Mine. Theirs. So that we can look at each other as men, women... humans. Without making any distinction.

I want to salute the exceptional work of director Sylvain Scott on the original version of this show. We created this text together, and you can read him everywhere between these lines. I was also excited and deeply proud to see our Margaret and William come to life in Stratford, under the direction of Esther Jun and her amazing team. Theatre is sometimes a series of accidents that create new meaning. Now I feel as if my characters themselves have orchestrated everything, without me even realizing it, so that they could be here with you in these pages. And I love them for that: they have found their own way to you.

Finally, a huge thank you to the fabulous Leanna Brodie, who has accompanied me for almost ten years. She translates my plays the way one silently understands another's heart. She has, and will long continue to have, my full confidence. She is a magnificent accident, and one of the most beautiful, on my journey as a writer.

— Rébecca Déraspe

Translator's Notes

Rébecca Déraspe is one of the leading playwrights of her generation in the vibrant French-language theatre culture of the province of Québec. This is our fourth collaboration, after *You Are Happy* (produced in Ottawa, Chicago, and Edmonton, and published by Playwrights Canada Press), *Gametes*, and *The Lessons*. I am also fortunate to work with several writers of Rébecca's cohort, translating their plays from the rich, often earthy expressiveness of Québécois French into my native Canadian English. They are a phenomenal group of artists. I adore the precision and muscularity of their dialogue; their fearless humour; their unbridled theatrical imaginations. I think that what makes Rébecca unique is her humane yet sparkling comic vision, the way her glorious wit interacts with her fierce feminism and a deep well of authentic emotion. Just like Shakespeare's characters, those of Déraspe feel things profoundly and passionately and express them immediately and accurately...but as in Shakespeare, the intensity of their desires and the rhythmic pull of the language ensure that they can't just lie there wallowing in their feelings. Not while there are songs to be sung and deeds to be done!

Whereas Sylvain Scott's original vision was notable for its elegant theatricality and sparkling wit, what I found especially compelling about Esther Jun's vision of *I Am William* was the way in which she connected the dots...for example, between exceptional women who get buried by the cultures they live in, and the many kinds of people who have long been denied the chance to make a full contribution to society.

I am reminded of the current *New York Times* series Overlooked. When that newspaper's editors realized that their obituaries overwhelmingly celebrated the accomplishments of straight white men, they started going back through their vaults to see who they had missed. It turns out that the range of omissions is astonishing! As I read these freshly unearthed stories, I keep thinking of all the people who have long needed to hear them, whether to have their biases challenged or their hope and ambition renewed.

When I was a young aspiring writer, my teachers and peers would sometimes use Shakespeare as a weapon: "If women writers are so great," they would cry, "how come there are no female Shakespeares?" You will hear Rébecca's answer to that very problematic question in this play. My answer is: I don't know... I only know that we're lucky there is one Rébecca Déraspe.

— Leanna Brodie

Translator's Acknowledgements

Thanks to Sylvain Scott and his gifted team; Théâtre Le Clou, which commissioned my translation as well as the original play; Emma Tibaldo and Playwrights Workshop Montréal for their essential workshop of my translation; my Vancouver writing group, The Pod (Carmen Aguirre, Elaine Avila, Lucia Frangione, Meghan Gardiner, Shawn Macdonald, and my beloved spouse Jovanni Sy) for ongoing support; and Esther Jun and her wonderful team at the Stratford Festival... especially her musical director and our mutual friend Kong Kie Njo, who went far above and beyond in order to help me render Rébecca, Benoit, and Chloé's glorious songs in English.

Foreword

I Am William is a joyous romp through Elizabethan England that turns the myth of Shakespeare on its head. I personally love the Bard and can safely say his plays have changed my life. The deification of him, however—especially at a time when many theatres in the country are attempting to decolonize the canon—has left a bitter taste in many a student's mouth. I sincerely hope this play can change that.

I had the great honour and privilege of bringing Rébecca Déraspe's play to English-speaking Canada.

As I do with all the plays I direct, I began to deep-dive into many research topics circling this play—Tudor England, the rise of Elizabeth I, the Shakespeare family history and the ENDLESS conspiracy theories surrounding authorship. What did I discover? Firstly, that questions of authorship inevitably marginalized Shakespeare himself. Most theories are based on the belief that a boy not born of the nobility could not possibly have been educated enough to write such incredible stories. Stories that are full of exotic locales, complicated plots, and noble ideals, and more importantly, reveal the contradictions of the human condition with such poetry and poignancy. History, Rébecca, and I, myself, say *"Non."* That is B.S. It does not matter where you come from. We are all a part of humankind and have our own narratives, our own stories. Anyone can write their stories down. Anyone can change the world with their life.

My second discovery was that, in the long run, none of my research really mattered. *I Am William* is creating an alternative history. Besides the subjugation of women, there is no historical basis to the main story of this play. Rébecca used her imagination. She inserted herself into the story because that is what writers do. She wrote this play so children, especially those who felt unseen, unheard, and unable to speak out can feel empowered to write their own stories. What if…a girl wrote all those plays? What if…I could write plays like that? What if…I picked up a pen (or more appropriately started typing) and wrote about my life?

What would happen? Maybe nothing. Maybe everything! And in between those unknowns is the pure wonderment and hope of youth. That is where imagination, fairies and *I Am William* live.

— Esther Jun
March 2022

Esther Jun is the Director of the Langham Directors' Workshop and Artistic Associate for Planning at the Stratford Festival.

Production History

Rébecca Déraspe's *Je suis William* premiered at Théâtre du Vieux-Terrebonne on Nov. 2, 2017, in a production by Théâtre Le Clou, under the artistic direction of Monique Gosselin, Sylvain Scott, and Benoît Vermeulen.

Cast:

Margaret: Édith Arvisais

William: Simon Labelle-Ouimet

Mary, John, Elizabeth, The Earl of Leicester: Renaud Paradis

Director / Choreographer / Set Designer: Sylvain Scott

Assistant Director: Dominique Cuerrier

Musician: Benoit Landry

Costume Designer: Linda Brunelle

Composers: Benoit Landry, Chloé Lacasse

Lighting Designer: Luc Prairie

Dramaturg: Paul Lefebvre

Movement: Monik Vincent

Makeup: François Cyr

Chandelier Design and Build: Nathalie Trépanier

Wigs: Géraldine Courchesne

A developmental reading of Leanna Brodie's translation *I Am William* was held on May 3, 2018, by Playwrights Workshop Montreal. The actors were Kym Dominique-Ferguson, Patrick Keeler, and Sarah Segal-Lazar, and the director was Emma Tibaldo.

Théâtre Le Clou premiered *I Am William* on Nov. 17, 2018, as part of the Coups de théâtre festival, featuring the same creative team as *Je suis William*. Additional music and lyrics for this production were provided by Ariane Bisson McLernon. *Je suis William* was commissioned, developed, and produced by

Théâtre Le Clou. Leanna Brodie's translation was commissioned by Théâtre Le Clou.

A revised and expanded version of Rébecca Déraspe's *I Am William* premiered at the Stratford Festival, under the artistic direction of Antoni Cimolino, on Aug. 14, 2021.

Cast:

Margaret: Shakura Dickson

William: Landon Doak

Mary, Elizabeth: Shannon Taylor

John, The Earl of Leicester: Allan Louis

Director: Esther Jun

Assistant Director: Sadie Epstein-Fine

Translator (Book and Lyrics): Leanna Brodie

Composers: Benoit Landry, Chloé Lacasse

Musical Director/Keyboards: Kong Kie Njo

Musicians: Graham Hargrove, Ben Bolt-Martin

Sound Designer: Maddie Bautista

Set and Costume Designers: Michelle Bohn

and Samantha McCue

Lighting: Arun Srinivasan

Dramaturg: Kamana Ntibarikure

Choreographer: Alyssa Martin

Stage Manager: Kat Chin

Assistant Stage Manager: Madison Kalbhenn

Apprentice Stage Manager: Scarlett Larry

"The family gathers round…" (Shannon Taylor, Shakura Dickson, Landon Doak, Allan Louis) Photo by David Hou for the Stratford Festival.

"Sister. You're amazing." (Shakura Dickson, Landon Doak) Photo by David Hou for the Stratford Festival.

"The roosters rise and shine…" (Shannon Taylor, Allan Louis, Landon Doak) Photo by David Hou for the Stratford Festival.

"Margaret, how I wish to see things through your eyes…" (Shakura Dickson, Shannon Taylor) Photo by David Hou for the Stratford Festival.

"That's the ecstasy of a crowd on seeing the Queen enter the theatre."
(Shannon Taylor) Photo by David Hou for the Stratford Festival.

William (Landon Doak) and Margaret (Shakura Dickson), the
Shakespeare twins. Photo by David Hou for the Stratford Festival.

Margaret Shakespeare (Édith Arvisais) considers her options. Photo by François Godard for Théâtre Le Clou.

When John Shakespeare comes home from work, his children do whatever they can to stay out of his way. (Édith Arvisais, Simon Labelle-Ouimet, Renaud Paradis) Photo by François Godard for Théâtre Le Clou.

William Shakespeare (Simon Labelle-Ouimet) woos his first crush. Photo by François Godard for Théâtre Le Clou.

John Shakespeare comforts his heartbroken son William. (Renaud Paradis, Simon Labelle-Ouimet) Photo by François Godard for Théâtre Le Clou.

Mary Shakespeare struggles to understand her complicated daughter Margaret. (Renaud Paradis, Édith Arvisais) Photo by François Godard for Théâtre Le Clou.

Elizabeth I makes the twins an offer. (Renaud Paradis, Édith Arvisais, Simon Labelle-Ouimet) Photo by François Godard for Théâtre Le Clou.

Characters

MARGARET SHAKESPEARE (Age 13)

WILLIAM SHAKESPEARE (Age 13)

NARRATOR

JOHN (Father to the Shakespeare twins)

MARY (Mother to the Shakespeare twins)

THE EARL OF LEICESTER

ELIZABETH I

THE WITCH-HUNTERS

THE ROOSTERS

Notes from the translator on the version and format

This version of the script was conceived for four performers. The original version for three performers, as developed and produced by Théâtre le Clou, omits some material for the character of MARY.

Song lyrics are indented and capitalized, except for the Prologue and Epilogue, which are spoken with underscoring rather than sung.

1 – Prologue

NARRATOR:
Once upon a long ago
And far far away
Like a century or five or so before today
On a distant shore
On England's green and pleasant plain
Came a ninja who kills with a quill, a mutant whose powers will scramble your brain
A child is born, a cry is heard
Words form and storm the heights in flights like mighty birds
William Shakespeare is here, the King of Poet Nation
The Kendrick of the iambic, Avon assassin amassing reputation
Romeo Juliet Othello Hamlet
His rhymes amaze, his rhythm grabs
Whether you're a girl in love, or just an old dude with no abs
As he conquers the planet consuming the stage with the rage of his powerful beats
The Goodnight Sweet Prince of slick theatrical feats
His verses like icebreakers
Smash a passage through all the years

William the founder William the master
William also had a sister

As this play's narrator,
Articulator of glory
Watch me mash up and crash up this hero's origin story
What's the truth
What's the lie
What's certain is we're born we die then curtain
Between the two I'm telling you History the way I wish it was
Between me and you, that's what everybody does
The lies you want to believe in are written right here on my skin
And even if my depiction is fiction
I swear to you, this story is ours too
It's true, even in its fantasy, its spin
It's all true
Let's begin

Scene 1

> *1577. Stratford, England.*
>
> *WILLIAM, MARGARET, and JOHN are strolling down the path through the woods, at night. The starry sky is magnificent.*

JOHN:
Oh! What a lush English forest. In the age in which we live—since this is 1577 and you are both thirteen years old—what happened to you this evening was —

WILLIAM:
Spectaculicious!

JOHN:
That's right: spectacular.

WILLIAM:
Exceptionalistical!

JOHN:
That's right: exceptional.

WILLIAM:
Extraordinatious!

JOHN:
Calm down, William.

WILLIAM:
I can't.

JOHN:
Just breathe.

WILLIAM:
She was barely a few feet away. A few little feet. I could even see a bit of the sparkly train of her Queen of England dress. I, William Shakespeare, caught a glimpse of the Royal Fabric. Can you believe it?

MARGARET:
Look at the stars.

WILLIAM:
Can you believe it?

MARGARET:
They're magnificent.

WILLIAM:
Can you?

MARGARET:
I would love to attach my eyes to one of them and observe the cartography of the human race.

JOHN:
(*Aside.*) And it is here, at this very moment, at this exact second, that the problems begin. (*To Margaret.*) What was that, you little brat?

MARGARET:
I said: Oh-stars-now-give-me-something-to-wash-so-that-I-may-rejoice.

WILLIAM:
And what can one say of the play put on by the Earl? The actors were amazing: completely present on stage, yet at the same time propelled by invisible wings that made them seem taller than they are.

JOHN:
It was not bad, son: I'm with you there. Not bad at all.

WILLIAM:
One was a knight! The other a king! There was love! And weeping! They are unspeakably lucky.

MARGARET:
You have more talent than all of those actors put together, brother. You know that.

WILLIAM:
You think? Do you really believe that? Really truly?

MARGARET:
Of course. You were playing comedy and tragedy for me when we were still in Mamma's womb. If I were a rich, powerful, respected earl, I would propel you onto all the stages in the world.

WILLIAM holds MARGARET to his heart.

So. What shall we do as we wait for you to start breathing again? Shall we revolutionize the world? Shall we do great deeds?

JOHN:
You, missy, are going home.

WILLIAM:
She can stay with us. She's fine with us.

JOHN:
Your mother needs you.

MARGARET:
But Papa—

JOHN:
"But" in the mouth of a girl is a sound that scratches men's ears.

WILLIAM:
It doesn't scratch mine!

JOHN:
Let us walk hither, my precious son. We shall recite poetry; we shall learn to lift up enormous tree-trunks; I shall open my heart to you about the time when I was the mayor of this city, and reveal the financial troubles swamping my glove-making business and poised to cause my ruin.

WILLIAM:
>Oh, look over there, Papa. Some very rare birds in the distance, beckoning you closer.

JOHN:
>Oh yeah?

WILLIAM:
>I think they are some very kind little fairies who wish to give you advice about your crumbling fortune.

JOHN:
>Great! I shall run towards them, because we live in an age when people still believe in fairies.

>>*JOHN runs off, looking in vain for the "little fairies."*

MARGARET:
>What are you talking about?!

WILLIAM:
>A little farther, Papa.

MARGARET:
>But—

WILLIAM:
>I need to make sure he can't overhear our conversation.

JOHN:
>Little fairies!

MARGARET:
>What conversation?

WILLIAM:
>Are you going to come and hide under the classroom window tomorrow?

MARGARET:
>Yes, if I can finish my chores before sunset.

WILLIAM:
We've got philosophy and I don't understand a thing. You can explain the parts I don't get.

MARGARET:
Shush. Papa might hear you. I'll be there.

JOHN:
Well, I don't see any birds or fairies.

WILLIAM and MARGARET burst out laughing.

JOHN:
Margaret Shakespeare? What are you still doing here? Who will prepare my footbath, salted with the salt of your sweat? Off to the house with you.

WILLIAM:
(*Whispering.*) See you tomorrow.

2 – *Unfair!*

MARGARET:
IT'S SO UNFAIR
INCREDIBLY UNFAIR
LIKE I'M
NOT EVEN THERE
"GO JOIN YOUR MUM"
"GO SWEEP THE STAIR"
MY LIFE IS SO UNFAIR

IT'S SO UNFAIR
INCREDIBLY UNFAIR
LIKE I'M
NOT EVEN THERE
HE'S LIKE A KING
I'M JUST A THING
MY LIFE IS SO UNFAIR

IT'S SO UNFAIR
INCREDIBLY UNFAIR
LIKE I'M
NOT EVEN THERE

"YOU ARE A GIRL
HE IS THE TOP
HE GETS THE WORLD
YOU GET A MOP"
WHY IS IT SO UNFAIR?

Scene 2

At the Shakespeare home.

MARY:

We're at the Shakespeare home and now the roosters rise and shine!

3 – *The Roosters (1)*

THE ROOSTERS:
IT'S TRUE!
WE COCK-A-DOODLE-DO!
LA LA LA LA LA LA LA!

MARY:

(*Calling.*) Up and at 'em! Latin isn't learned lying down. It's learned with bottom-spanking and repetition. Up, William! Bottoms were created so men could be educated! Not for them to lounge on! Get up!

> *MARGARET runs on. She's carrying a pile of clothing, a stack of cauldrons, several cakes, and a roasted pig.*

MARGARET:

I've completed my tasks for the day! May I go for a stroll?

MARY:

(*Calling.*) William! I said get up!

MARGARET:

Mamma my Mamma?

MARY:

What? Yes? Who? Where?

MARGARET:

Here, hidden beneath my already-finished chores.

MARY:

(*Calling.*) William Shakespeare! Are you waiting for your mother to get you out of bed by splashing chicken soup on you?

MARGARET:

Mamma my Mamma?

MARY:

Oh, Margaret. My poor child.

MARGARET:

Poor? Child?

MARY:

Put all this down and sit. It's about the Gilborne girl.

MARGARET:

Benedicta?

MARY:

Yes. Benedicta. It's bad. It was the talk of the market this morning. Did you know she could read and write?

MARGARET:

...

MARY:

The witch-hunters suspected her of sorcery because she was boasting in the village that she had read all of Homer. Girls are banned from school, so how could she know how to read? Last night, they tied her to a chair and dropped the chair in the water. They waited to see if she'd manage to free herself… That's their way of finding out if evil has found a home in the soul of a poor village girl. Those who escape the knotted ropes are clearly aided by the devil. So, they hang them in the public square.

MARGARET:

And?

MARY:

She couldn't free herself.

MARGARET:
   And?

MARY:
   She drowned.

4 – *The Witch-Hunters*

THE WITCH-HUNTERS:
MARGARET, WE ARE WATCHING, WE
KNOW WHERE YOU GO
HANG YOU UP ON HIGH OR DROWN YOU
DOWN BELOW

RUN, YOU CANNOT HIDE, WE KNOW YOU
RUN TO SCHOOL
PRESSED AGAINST THE WALL YOU HEAR
IT ALL, YOU FOOL

MARGARET, WE ARE WATCHING, WE
KNOW WHERE YOU GO
BURN YOU AT THE STAKE OR DROWN
YOU DOWN BELOW

WE KNOW THAT YOU DO KNOW HOW TO
READ AND WRITE
SO BEWARE, WE'RE GOING TO COME FOR
YOU ONE NIGHT
SO PREPARE, WE'RE GOING TO COME FOR
YOU ONE NIGHT

MARGARET, WE ARE WATCHING, WE
KNOW WHERE YOU GO
MARGARET, WE ARE WATCHING, WE
KNOW WHERE YOU GO
MARGARET, WE ARE WATCHING, WE
KNOW WHERE YOU GO

MARY:
   Are you all right, dear child? Are you thinking or crying?

MARGARET:
They are pigs.

MARY:
Hush. Someone might hear you. Your hurt and anger have the right to exist, but in silence. William Shakespeare! Get up or I shall behead a living thing in your bed!

WILLIAM:
Coming, Mamma my Mamma. Coming.

MARY:
Off with you to grammar school.

WILLIAM:
I love you so much, Mamma.

MARY:
We'll discuss your Oedipus complex some other time.

WILLIAM:
Cut it out, Mamma. You know I'm in love with Amuletta.

MARY:
Forget about her: we could never afford to marry into that family.

> *WILLIAM leaves the house.*

WILLIAM:
(*Whispering to MARGARET.*) See you soon.

> *MARGARET turns away, her face twisted with pain and fury.*

You've changed your mind.

MARGARET:
They drowned Benedicta for knowing how to read. What will they do to me, William? Never again shall I crouch beneath that window to learn words that could be my undoing.

WILLIAM:
That's dreadful.

MARGARET:
Yes, it is. But it's only the banal reminder of ordinary life.
Promise me that you'll never be one of those faithless men
who banish the intelligence of women by drowning them.

WILLIAM:
If anyone were about to do you harm, I would fling myself
before the flames of his rage. Look, like this.

> *He pretends to battle enormous enemies in order to
> make his sister laugh. He suddenly stops and looks
> at someone passing by.*

MARGARET:
Sure, you'll fling yourself... unless you spy Amuletta in the
distance.

MARY:
Go on, boy!

WILLIAM:
I'm dead serious, sister. I will protect you from—

MARY:
I can see your head, and I swear, if you do not run to school
this instant, I'm sending a lion to bite you on the bum!

Scene 3

The Shakespeares' kitchen. Evening. The family has just had dinner.

MARY:
Good work on the split pea soup, daughter my daughter. Now just clear, clean, and rinse.

MARGARET:
Yes, Mamma my Mamma.

WILLIAM:
Could I maybe help her?

MARY:
I'm sorry, what did you say?

WILLIAM:
I said, I could clean and rinse?

MARY:
If your father heard that, your ears would be bright red and half pulled off your head. With his business almost bankrupt, the last thing he needs is more bad news... like a son who wants to be a kitchen maid. I'm going to go scrub the tub so you can wash certain parts of your body before putting them to bed. "A good sleep waters the wits." Or... something.

She goes out.

MARGARET:
Play me that scene again instead: the one where the brave knight runs his enemy through the heart with a breadstick, to save his beloved Amuletta from the hands of—

WILLIAM:
I love her.

MARGARET:
I know. I know.

WILLIAM:
I'm so sad Father and Mother can't provide for our union.

MARGARET:
Sad? Why so sad?

WILLIAM:
I love her.

MARGARET:
Then you have only to say so. Stand up tall before her. Lift up your head. And tell her everything! Tell her: I love you, Amuletta, and my arms shall be your home.

WILLIAM:
That's wonderful. "My arms shall be your home." Wonderful.

MARGARET:
You need to play up your intelligence. And your sense of humour.

WILLIAM:
Sister. You're amazing.

MARGARET:
Hush. Papa is—

5 – Papa Is Home

JOHN:
PAPA IS HOME PAPA

MARGARET AND WILLIAM:
LET US HUSH
LET US HUSH

JOHN:
THROUGH ALL THE WORKING DAY
I TOIL MY WEARY WAY

MARGARET AND WILLIAM:
LET US BRING HIM SUPPER
AND LET HIM GO TO BED

JOHN:
THE TRADER WITH NO TRADE
ALL IS LOST, ALL IS GONE

MARGARET AND WILLIAM:
PAPA OUR PAPA
PAPA

JOHN:
GOODNIGHT, CHILDREN
GOODNIGHT

MARGARET AND WILLIAM:
YES, WE LOVE YOU DEARLY
PAPA

JOHN:
GOODNIGHT

WILLIAM:
I liked it better when he was like what he was like before. Losing everything doesn't mean you have to be such a misery about it.

MARGARET:
He once was the mayor: now he just begs.

WILLIAM:
He once was a player: now he... lays eggs?

MARGARET:
Lays eggs?

WILLIAM:
Has six legs?

MARGARET:
Quaffs the dregs?

WILLIAM:
Whats the *whats*?!

MARGARET:
His sadness robs this house of its right to light.

WILLIAM:
Yes. That.

MARGARET:
Like a king to whom eternal glory has been promised, from whom all has been snatched at one fell swoop.
"Take now my life, of which remains alone
The torn remembrance of my stolen crown."

WILLIAM:
(*After a kingly pause.*) "...the torn remembrance of my stolen crown."

MARGARET:
Well. Go on. Goodnight.

WILLIAM:
Me too, Margaret.

MARGARET:
You mean, "You, too."

WILLIAM:
No: I'm angry, too. Like you, I'm boiling with the injustice of it all. And if I could give you arms to battle by my side, I myself would armsificate you.

MARGARET:
I would arm you.

WILLIAM:
That's what I just said.

MARGARET:
Stop. Save your fancy words to write to Amuletta.

MARY:
William! Bath-time!

Scene 4

Night. MARGARET is in the attic, surrounded by pages and pages of writing.

6 – Now, As Others Are Sleeping

MARGARET:
NOW, AS OTHERS ARE SLEEPING
I'M HIDDEN AWAY
IN MY MIND I'VE BEEN KEEPING
MY SONNETS, MY SECRETS
I WRITE WITH EV'RYTHING I HAVE

THE LOVER (MALE):
For never shall I rest by day or night

MARGARET:
I WRITE FOR EV'RYTHING I LOVE

THE LOVER (MALE):
But upright as an oak tree brave the storm
Till Jove's own lightning cleave its trunk in twain

MARGARET:
MY PEN IS SHARPER THAN A SWORD
MY RAGE ON EVERY PAGE IS POURED

THE LOVER (MALE):
And even with my blood shall I avenge
What scorn and strain they rain upon our love

MARGARET:
IN THE NIGHT THERE IS FREEDOM
TO BE WHO I AM
FINDING COMFORT IN STORIES
OF STAR-CROSSED LOVERS
I WRITE WITH EV'RYTHING I HAVE

THE LOVER (FEMALE):
Never could I see thee shed one bead
Of blood, without I stoop to gather it
Each single droplet like a precious rose

MARGARET:
I WRITE FOR EV'RYTHING I LOVE

THE LOVER (FEMALE):
I'll vent my fury on their luckless sails

MARGARET:
MY PEN IS SHARPER THAN A SWORD
MY RAGE ON EVERY PAGE IS POURED

THE LOVER (FEMALE):
I'll stay, and never shalt thou be forlorn

MARGARET:
AND THOUGH DEATH AND DESPAIR
HUNT ME OUT THERE
IT'S PEACEFUL
ALONE HERE

THE LOVER (MALE):
Put on men's garb and all shall follow thee
Which art more high majestic than an alpine peak
The heavens curtsy to thy star-bright eyes
My Benedicta

MARGARET:
Thee I shall avenge
Until

MARGARET falls asleep over her papers. The light goes out.

Scene 5

> *Morning. WILLIAM and MARGARET are asleep:*
> *she in the attic; he, guitar in hand, in his room.*

MARY:
 Up and at 'em, children! Hark, the roosters crow!

7 – *The Roosters (2)*

THE ROOSTERS:
IT'S TRUE!
WE COCK-A-DOODLE-DO!

MARGARET:
 What? Already?

MARY:
 Up up up! I'm clap-clap-clapping my hands!

WILLIAM:
 (*Calling from his bedroom.*) I'm coming, Mamma: I was so inspired, I was up all night! I wrote! I wrote so much!

> *MARGARET runs into the kitchen.*

MARGARET:
 Morning, Mamma-Mamma!

MARY:
 You were up bright and early. I came to your room, but you weren't there.

MARGARET:
 Because the fields are so beautiful at dawn?

MARY:
 Did you hear what your brother just told me?

MARGARET:
 What? About what?

MARY:
About night and writing—

MARGARET:
Huh? What are you uh—that's—I'm—

MARY:
He's writing. Your brother is writing. If I weren't restraining myself, I'd be drumming on the furniture for joy.

> *WILLIAM enters, visibly exhausted, but happy. He proudly holds his guitar.*

WILLIAM:
Ladies, have a seat. Allow me to present to you what I have prepared for Amuletta. Do I look handsome when I strike this pose?

MARGARET:
You think Amuletta will be overwhelmed by the charms of a pose?

WILLIAM:
Of course!

MARGARET:
You really don't understand girls.

WILLIAM:
I'm too skinny, is that it?

MARY:
What are you talking about, Margaret? Stop acting like a feminist. That's very bad. Besides, in the age in which we live, I'm not supposed to know that word.

WILLIAM:
I wrote a song and you want to hear it.

MARGARET:
Really?

WILLIAM:

It was very hard to choose between making it about stars, or things that rhyme with "etta." See if you can guess what I decided to get her.

8 – Amuletta (1)

WILLIAM:
OH AMULETTA
YOU'RE SO GREAT THAT NO ONE IS EVER BETTER
YOU ARE NOT A SILENT LETTER
YOU ARE NOT AN IRISH SETTER
YOU ARE NOT A CHUNK OF CHEDDAR
YOU'RE THE GIRL I CAN'T FORGET-AH

MARGARET:
It's—

WILLIAM:
Tell me, tell me.

MARGARET:
It's—

WILLIAM:
I know: it's awesome!

MARY:
(*Running off.*) John! Our son is a genius!

Scene 6

9 – Amuletta (2)

WILLIAM:
I'M DRESSING UP RIGHT
I'M LOOKING MY BEST
I'M READY I'M SET
I'M PASSING THIS TEST

OUT IN THE GARDEN
I PICK HER A ROSE
AND LILAC AND JASMINE
FOR THE EYES AND THE NOSE

AS I WALK TO HER HOUSE
I'M A MAN NOW AT LAST
YES, IT'S ME, GIRL: THAT BOY
YOU'VE BEEN WALKING RIGHT PAST

KNOCK KNOCK KNOCK ON HER DOOR
BANG BANG BANG, COME TO ME
BOOM BOOM BOOM GOES MY HEART
STARS ARE ALL THAT I SEE

WILLIAM:

Amuletta, I'm madly in love with you please accept this bouquet of flowers so your eyes may brighten my days and my nights and the mornings we will spend together. Make me the man I always thunk—thinked? thank? thought!—I could be. My arms shall be at home!

WILLIAM:
I DREAM OF YOU, OF YOUR EYES, OF
YOUR FACE
I WILL BE YOUR KING
YOU, MY EVERYTHING
COME ON WITH ME
COME AND JOIN IN THE PARADE
THE GREAT PARADE OF LOVE

Silence. Then WILLIAM howls with pain. MARGARET runs in.

MARGARET:

What's wrong, brother? Are you hurt? Did you step on a nail?

WILLIAM:

She laughed at me! She asked, "Where's the parade?"... And then she started tapping her thighs the way you'd tap a baby to make him belch. Margaret! My heart is devastated!

MARGARET:

I can see that. I can see that quite clearly.

WILLIAM:

I'm going to sink into this pile of straw and suffer. Howl! Howl! Howl! How can you stand to see me suffer like this? Without lifting a finger to save me from my intestinal agony?

MARGARET:

I'm sorry, brother. I don't know how. I don't know. What. To do. To.

WILLIAM:

I tried to reap her heart and instead I reaped her scorn. Howl!

10 – A Heart

MARGARET:
A HEART
IS NOT FOR YOU TO REAP

A HEART
IS TO CHERISH, NOT TO KEEP
NOT A THING YOU CAN OWN

A HEART
CAN BLOOM IF LEFT ALONE

WILLIAM:

Why are you smiling and staring at the sky while I'm spilling my guts here?

MARGARET:
Who? Me?

WILLIAM:
I tell you, sister: this pain wracking my body is worse than any from blade of knife. Papa! Mamma! It hurts too much!

JOHN comes running in.

JOHN:
What's wrong, son my son?

WILLIAM:
I'm infected with love!

JOHN:
Oh no! Not love!

WILLIAM:
Yes, Papa!

JOHN:
Did a witch do this to you?

MARGARET:
Witches don't exist, Papa. They're simply what men invented in order to safeguard their imaginary supremacy.

JOHN and WILLIAM:
What is she talking about?!

Scene 7

> *In WILLIAM's room, a few days later. Night.*
> *MARGARET enters very quietly.*

11 – Twins

> MARGARET:
> YOUR SADNESS BREAKS MY HEART
> I FEEL IT IN MY SOUL

MARGARET:
William. William, it's me.

WILLIAM:
Who what you who?

MARGARET:
Shhh.

WILLIAM:
You woke me up to tell me not to talk?

MARGARET:
I woke you up *and* I'm telling you not to talk. I have something for you. These past few days, you've been under the impression that I was indifferent to your anguish. Rest assured that nothing could be more false. I remained locked in my silence precisely because I was engaged in sounding in the depths of myself all the sorrow that beset your spirit.

> MARGARET:
> YOUR SADNESS BREAKS MY HEART
> I FEEL IT IN MY SOUL

MARGARET:
You know that Benedicta's death and Papa's troubles afflict me. And this love that tortures you dismays me, too. But each night I am transported, William. Go on and read what I've written. It's a play. I've filled it with all my love for you.

I hope to make your heart dream, for dreams, especially waking ones, have power to heal all wounds. I love you, brother. Did you just fall asleep?

WILLIAM:

...

MARGARET:
You fell asleep.

> *MARGARET lays her play beside WILLIAM. She leaves the room.*

> MARGARET:
> AND NOW YOUR STORM IS PASSED
> AND NOW I'LL SLEEP AT LAST

Scene 8

The Shakespeares' dining table, a few days later.

12 – The Family

THE COMPANY:
THE TABLE NOW IS SET
THE FAM'LY GATHERS ROUND
OUR PLATES ARE PILED UP HIGH
OUR DAY WITH JOY IS CROWNED

THE ROAST THAT GLEAMS WITH FAT
THE BREAD THAT NOW IS BLESSED
OF ALL THE RICH REPAST
OUR LAUGHTER IS THE BEST

AND EVEN FATHER SMILES
AS IN THE OLDEN DAYS
FOR FOOD'S THE MUSIC OF LOVE
AND EV'RYBODY PLAYS

THE MEN WENT OFF TO LEARN
THE WOMEN WERE THE COOKS
FOR THIS THE MEN DID YEARN
WHILE STUCK BEHIND THEIR BOOKS

LET'S STAY HERE FOR ALL TIME
A GALLANT WARRIOR CREW
FOR WHEN WE'RE SIDE BY SIDE
THERE'S NOTHING WE CAN'T DO

JOHN:
Settle down, everyone. Papa here would like to give thanks to our Lord for giving our William his smile again.

MARY:
Mamma would like to give thanks, too. Our William is quite handsome when he's beaming at a pork roast.

WILLIAM:
That's not the Lord's doing, parents my parents. It's—

MARGARET:
Bon appétit!

MARY:
Whose doing is it, then?

WILLIAM:
It's—

MARGARET:
Delicious pork with onions!

MARY:
Who?

WILLIAM:
It's—

MARGARET:
Delicious potatoes with potatoes!

MARY:
Whose is it? Who?

WILLIAM:
It's—

MARGARET:
Extra-super-delicious water with water!

JOHN:
Margaret! Enough! Let your brother speak.

13 – *Beat, My Heart*

MARGARET:
BEAT MY HEART BEAT MY HEART BEAT
BEAT MY HEART BEAT MY HEART BEAT
BEAT MY HEART BEAT MY HEART BEAT
BEAT MY HEART BEAT MY HEART BEAT

WILLIAM:
Exactly, Papa.

JOHN:
Exactly, Papa?

WILLIAM:
Exactly, Mamma.

MARY:
Exactly, Mamma?

WILLIAM:
We need to let Margaret speak.

JOHN:
What what what do I hear?

WILLIAM:
You hear the voice of your son telling you to hear the voice of your daughter, for the voice of your daughter rings out stronger than—

MARGARET:
I promise, Papa. I won't say another word, Papa my Papa. I simply wanted the cooks around the table to be praised for the preparation of this sublime refection. However, I should have awaited the advent of silence before bestowing my *Bravissimo*.

JOHN:
"Bestowing my *Bravissimo*"?

MARY:
What does she want to stow? Where does she want to stow it?

WILLIAM:
Do you hear that? She's a poet! Your daughter is a remarkable poet!

JOHN:
She's a poet? My daughter is a remarkable poet?

MARY:
I'm not stowing anything around here!

MARGARET:
I'm not a poet! I am not a remarkable poet!

JOHN:
Wait. Who's saying what?

MARY:
I'm saying, this house is stuffed to the rafters as is.

MARGARET:
And I'm saying William is tired. So tired. A fatigue that makes one fear the worst. Let me touch his forehead: Oh! This child is ill! Did not you see the suffering concealed behind this pasty visage?

WILLIAM:
Me?

MARGARET:
You're very sick, William.

WILLIAM:
I'm very sick?

MARGARET:
Absolutely. You are cadaverously pale.

WILLIAM:
Me? Pale? Perfectly pale?

MARGARET:
You almost burn my retinas.

WILLIAM:
Actually, I don't feel too good.

MARY:
Should I arrange for a bloodletting?

WILLIAM:
No!

MARY:
Or just run around the kitchen yelling "The plague it's the plague."

MARGARET:
You should go lie down.

WILLIAM:
I've got the plague?

MARGARET:
I recommend immediate horizontality.

JOHN:
Stop talking and take him straight to his bed, Margaret.

MARGARET:
Yes, of course. Come, brother. Lean on me here, and here. Above all, not another word. Your throat is inflamed. I can hear it in your breathing. And you have a stuffy nose.

MARY:
Well, that doesn't sound like the plague.

WILLIAM:
But—

MARGARET:
Silence! Else death shall come for you right here, right in front of your family, right in front of the roast pig. Did you know that pigs are creatures that—

14 – Shut Up

JOHN:
SHUT UP
FATHER SAYS: OBEY!

SHUT UP
NOTHING MORE TO SAY

SHUT UP
YOUR PAPA'S HAD ENOUGH

SHUT UP
SHUT UP
SHUT UP

(*Aside.*) I know, I know: that was not very nice... but this is 1577, so girls are the property of their father and then of their husband. I'm within my rights to beat her if I want to. On the other hand...that would be kind of mean.

Scene 9

> *In WILLIAM's bedroom. MARGARET forces him to lie down.*

WILLIAM:

Sister my sister: am I going to die? I can see the scythe—Skith? Skythe?

MARGARET:

Scythe, yes, you were right the first time.

WILLIAM:

The scythe of Death—*la muerte!*—pointing its deadly blade at me. Am I going to die?

MARGARET:

Of course not, idiot.

WILLIAM:

Am I cured?

MARGARET:

That down there was theatre. You played your role very well. William, we need to talk.

WILLIAM:

OH! So that was just to get me out of the room! Death! Fever! It was all an act. You're brilliant, sister. Quite brilliant.

MARGARET:

I should never have given you my writing: it was a grave blunder.

WILLIAM:

You can't call those lines a "blunder." They're the most splendid things I've read in all my life. Margaret, I know fistfuls of men who would love to write as well as you. I'm part of that fistful myself. You saw how bad I write, right?

MARGARET:
Why did you try to denounce me down there? If Father and Mother found out I write, they would kill me. I thought I could trust you.

WILLIAM:
Father and Mother wouldn't kill you. Come on. Can you imagine Mamma with a—

MARGARET:
They would stop me writing. And stopping my writing would be like ending my life.

WILLIAM:
Uh, there's a bit of a difference.

MARGARET:
Writing is all I have, William. It allows me to escape this world and build new ones.

WILLIAM:
An actor you gave these words to would be the happiest of men, Margaret. I admire you so much it makes me tremble.

MARGARET:
Ask your teacher to give you some Sophocles and— Why did the blood just drain from your face?

WILLIAM:
I showed your writing to my teacher.

MARGARET:
Pardon me?

WILLIAM:
I showed your writing to my teacher.

MARGARET:
I heard you, but—I'm going to—I'm going to—

WILLIAM:

Look, I'm not stupid. I told him on the spot I made up those characters myself. I don't want you to be drowned. He wept. He said I was a demagogue.

MARGARET:

Demigod.

WILLIAM:

And I was going to leave it at that. But—

MARGARET:

But?

WILLIAM:

He sent it to the Earl of Leicester. You know, the one who produced that spectacle for the Queen? And I'm invited to meet him. Tomorrow. I won't go. Don't worry. I made up my mind a while ago. And then I forgot about it. It only came back to me just now as we were speaking. But let's change the subject! So, Margaret: how are things? Did you have a nice day?

MARGARET:

...

WILLIAM:

Cat got your tongue?

MARGARET:

...

WILLIAM:

You're not speaking. I'm listening and you're not speaking.

MARGARET:

From now on and forever more, YOU wrote those words. End of story. YOU are the author. Of. Those. Words.

WILLIAM:
I can't take credit for what doesn't belong to me. It'd be like stealing eggs and then saying, "Here are the eggs I laid," when everyone knows I'm not a chicken.

MARGARET:
Too. Late.

WILLIAM:
I repeat: I'm not going.

MARGARET:
Well then, he'll come and find you here. And he'll humiliate Papa and Mamma. And everyone will cry. You know these Lords and Earls! If you stand him up, you're insulting his power. So go to bed right away. You need to rest up for your big meeting tomorrow.

WILLIAM:
Do I really have to go?

MARGARET:
What world do you live in, William? If you disobey, you'll pay. Dearly.

WILLIAM:
Margaret.

MARGARET:
...

WILLIAM:
Margaret.

MARGARET:
...

15 – *Duet*

WILLIAM:
LOOK AT ME, SISTER
TRUST IN ME WHEN I SAY

I WON'T PUT YOU IN DANGER
I WON'T GIVE YOU AWAY

MARGARET:
STANDING HERE BEFORE ME
HOW DARE YOU TRY TO LIE
WHEN I SPEAK YOU IGNORE ME
IT'S YOUR FAULT IF I DIE

WILLIAM:
I ONLY WANTED TO SHARE
ALL THE THINGS THAT I FEEL
YOUR WORDS MAKE IT ALL REAL

MARGARET:
ONCE YOU GAVE ME A DREAM
AND NOW MY WRITING IS MY LIFE
BUT YOU HAVE THROWN IT ALL AWAY
HERE IN MY BACK I FEEL YOUR KNIFE
MY BROTHER BURIED ME TODAY

WILLIAM:
BUT I NEVER MEANT
TO HURT YOU
OR TO FAIL YOU
WHAT DO WE DO NOW?

Scene 10

> *MARGARET comes into the kitchen. MARY is*
> *alone at the table.*

MARY:
Is your brother feeling better, sweetheart?

MARGARET:
...

MARY:
You're breathing hard. Are you angry?

MARGARET:
...

MARY:
Are you cross at Papa your Papa?

MARGARET:
...

MARY:
He's tough on you sometimes. But he loves you so. He's afraid for you. You see, he can tell you don't accept the world as it is. And he fears lest you plunge headfirst into the dangerous pool of rebellion.

MARGARET:
...

MARY:
He's afraid you'll bring shame on our family with this questionable behaviour.

MARGARET:
Questionable behaviour? What does that mean? I do everything by the book. I hold my tongue; I hide my tears; I wash his clothes. Questionable behaviour? I could write and become the greatest author of all time, and still he would hate me, for women with the audacity to speak are witches who should have their heads cut off. Questionable

behaviour? When his sons get tangled in the slender thread of life, he lifts them up with all the love in his heart. Yet when a daughter of his says "no," she gets a faceful of his fury. And I'm the one with questionable behaviour?

MARY:

Don't cry. There, there. Don't cry. I didn't understand a word you just said, but stop crying.

MARGARET:

I know, I know: it's pointless. What's the use of trying to accomplish anything when everyone dreams of making our hair grow into the ground so that roots hold us in place until we die.

16 – Tell Me

MARGARET:
TELL ME
WHAT I MUST SCRAPE AND SCOUR
TELL ME
WHERE I MUST SCRUB THE STAIN
I'LL LIVE FROM HOUR TO HOUR
TELL ME
SO I'LL NEVER THINK AGAIN

TELL ME
HOW I MUST BOW AND BEND
TELL ME
WHAT I MUST HIDE AWAY
I DON'T WANT TO OFFEND
TELL ME
AND MY TEARS WILL END TODAY

TELL ME
WHAT I SHOULD SACRIFICE
TELL ME
I'LL DO AS YOU ADVISE
LEARN TO NOD AND BE NICE
TELL ME
HOW A WOMAN CAN SURVIVE

MARY:
I SAY
DAUGHTER, I LOVE YOU SO
I SAY
MORE THAN YOU COULD EVER KNOW
AS I'M WATCHING YOU GROW
I SAY
I WILL NEVER LET YOU GO

Scene 11

> *At the home of the EARL OF LEICESTER.*
> *WILLIAM enters his huge office.*

EARL OF LEICESTER:
  You!

WILLIAM:
  Yes!

EARL OF LEICESTER:
  Come in!

WILLIAM:
  Yes!

EARL OF LEICESTER:
  Sit down!

WILLIAM:
  Yes!

EARL OF LEICESTER:
  First of all, in one clear and precise word: Bravo. I was bowled over by your writing talent. I even exclaimed: "WHAT WRITING TALENT I AM BOWLED OVER." Your teacher did well to send me these dramatic scenes. Anyone else would have destroyed them on the spot. Certain nobles—I shall refrain from naming names—prefer to keep their money to finance enormous battles in the mud. It amuses them. But enough! I shall be brief and triumphant: William Shakespeare, will you be my protégé?

  It's simple. Quite simple. You write for me. I cover you with cash and you make plays whenever I want them and however I want them. If I say white, you write white. If I say red, you write red.

  You know, the Queen has long had a fondness for me, ever since I greeted her with a grandiose entertainment culminating in the appearance of a massive dolphin.

WILLIAM:

...

EARL OF LEICESTER:
No? Nothing?

WILLIAM:
It's just—

EARL OF LEICESTER:
Just just just?

WILLIAM:
Don't wanna.

EARL OF LEICESTER:
These words are the most potent I have ever laid eyes on.
This play promises a deafening success. Besides, the first
performance is a few days from now, in London.

WILLIAM:
You're saying... What?

EARL OF LEICESTER:
And you shall play the lead. The young maiden ready to
die for the boy she loves. Your teacher said that you are a
great actor, and you dream of being onstage.

WILLIAM:
No.

EARL OF LEICESTER:
I have also discovered that your father needs money. You
could pay all his debts and be the hero of your family.

WILLIAM:
No.

EARL OF LEICESTER:
You know a girl by the name of Amuletta?

WILLIAM:

...

EARL OF LEICESTER:
> A tiny bird told me you're quite sweet on her. But alas, the young maiden isn't all that interested in you.

WILLIAM:
> What?

EARL OF LEICESTER:
> By becoming WILLIAM SHAKESPEARE, you stand a much better chance in your amorous endeavours than by remaining williamshakespeare. Studies have shown that young women's main talent is for admiring the talent of others. And you can count on me to impress on her what a great artist you have become.

WILLIAM:
> May I please throw up on these important papers?

EARL OF LEICESTER:
> Of course not, William. You need to sign right here.

WILLIAM:
> You don't understand.

EARL OF LEICESTER:
> Are you telling me I don't understand?

WILLIAM:
> Yes, actually: I am telling you—

EARL OF LEICESTER:
> —If you refuse, your pretty head shall decorate my office wall. Do you understand that, William?

WILLIAM:
> Yes.

EARL OF LEICESTER:
> Go pack your little satchel. We leave for London tonight. Care for a donut?

17 – Run

CHORUS:
RUN AND RUN AND RUN AND RUN AND
RUN...

WILLIAM:
RAIN, RAIN, GO AWAY
DREAMS COME TRUE TODAY
I MADE A PROMISE
I MUSTN'T BETRAY

AN ACTOR ONSTAGE
A BIRD IN HIS CAGE
HE SAYS AMULETTA—
SO HE SAYS
SO HE SAYS

Scene 12

> *WILLIAM arrives at home, beside himself.*
> *MARGARET bars his way.*

MARGARET:
Tell me everything.

WILLIAM:
Out of my way.

MARGARET:
Did he hate it?

WILLIAM:
Out of my way.

MARGARET:
Tell me.

WILLIAM:
Leave me alone.

MARGARET:
You can't do what you're doing to me by doing what you're doing.

WILLIAM:
I can do as I please.

MARGARET:
This is all your fault. All of it. My desire to write: your fault. My play: your fault. The shame I feel in this moment: your fault. The least you could do is tell me what the Earl said about the words I gouged out of my heart with a knife. What did he say? They're laughable, is that it? I write like a baby?

WILLIAM:
Yes. That's right. He said he brought me there to tell me that the play is awful. And I shouldn't dare bother anyone else with such worthless drivel. Then he compared your

script to the bellowing of a calf that's about to keel over from sheer boredom. I was stupid. Stupid to see any merit in what you wrote.

MARY:
(*From the house.*) Margaret?

MARGARET:
...

MARY:
Margaret?

MARGARET:
...

MARY:
Margaret! Come help Mamma do every single thing around the house. The sun has already called it a day and we need to polish the cutlery.

> *MARGARET goes into the house. Her pain is too immense to be invisible. On seeing her, her mother takes her in her arms.*

MARY:
Not a word. Not a word. Go to bed.

> *MARGARET says nothing and disappears.*

WILLIAM:
What's with her?

MARY:
I rocked you both in the cradle. I took into my motherly heart all the hurt you could not hold back... and kissed your tear-swollen eyelids once you were calm again. But never have I seen such pain in the eyes of your sister. Never.

WILLIAM:
It's all my fault.

Scene 13

Night. The attic.

18 – The Scream in My Throat

MARGARET:
THE DAGGER OF THE NIGHT
CUTS DEEP INTO MY SOUL
I'M DROWNING IN MY SHAME
THE SCREAM IN MY THROAT

THE BREATH OF MY DISGRACE
THE BOMB INSIDE MY HEAD
SCATTERED FRAGMENTS OF MY PAIN
THE SCREAM IN MY THROAT

TEAR IT TO PIECES FOR ONCE AND FOR
ALL
TEAR ALL APART
I'LL BE THAT GIRL YOU ALL WANT ME TO
BE
AND TOIL THROUGH THE DAY WITH
JOYLESS HEART

THE RIVER OF MY GRIEF
FLOWS RED AND BLACK AND BLUE
MY WORDS HAVE BEEN MY SKIN
NOW THEY'RE MELTING INTO

THE SCREAM IN MY THROAT
THE SCREAM IN MY THROAT
THE SCREAM IN MY THROAT

William enters the attic. His satchel is ready.

WILLIAM:
I can hear you from my bedroom, sister. I hear it all. And I want to die in my stupid bed while packing my stupid satchel. Hearing you suffer hurts me more than the most burning burning of the most powerful flame. Especially since I'm holding the torch myself.

MARGARET:
What are you talking about?

WILLIAM:
That torch image, though? No? Nothing?

MARGARET:
It's not your fault that I'm ridiculous and Papa's pigs write better than me. Ridiculous Margaret.

WILLIAM:
Stop.

MARGARET:
Ridiculous Margaret ridiculous.

WILLIAM:
Stop it. You're astonishing. Each of your words contains all the contradictions of mankind. I look pathetic by your side. A dirty, lying brother who'd rather make up insults than have to tell you, admit to you, tell you—I'm off to London, Margaret.

MARGARET:
London? You'll get lost there!

WILLIAM:
The Earl said your words were the grandest things he's ever read.

MARGARET:
So you're saying...?

WILLIAM:
I'm saying I'm going to London because he wants me to act the words you wrote, onstage.

MARGARET:
Did you tell him I wrote those words?

WILLIAM:
Of course not.

MARGARET:
Promise me you'll keep my secret.

WILLIAM:
I don't understand, sister my sister. How can you stand to let me rob you of the acclaim you so richly deserve?

MARGARET:
I didn't write those words for praise or fame. I wrote them in order to exist, to heal myself, to make the world reveal itself to me. Not to reveal myself to the world.

WILLIAM:
You seem almost happy to see me go.

MARGARET:
I am—I am—I am. He really liked it?

WILLIAM:
Your smile is the most effective of remedies.

MARGARET:
It makes. Me. I. I'm. Just. I-want-to-dance-and-run-and-laugh-and-everything's-exploding-in-here-between-my-ears. I don't need his recognition. You've always dreamed of being an actor. I don't care about applause.

WILLIAM:
A few days from now, I'll be onstage. And I shall carry your words as one carries a precious baby who might die of cholera.

MARGARET:
Huh?

WILLIAM:
With pride! Goodbye, sister. Could you please take this to Amuletta tomorrow?

He gives her a letter and leaves.

MARGARET:

(*Reading the letter.*) "I love you, Amuletta. I'm off to London. But know that I carry with me the memory of your eyes, and the even brighter one of your smile. Know, too, that the story that will end up being whispered in your ear is not the only possible option. One day, I will explain."

He's learning, that brother of mine. He's learning.

Scene 14

*Night. WILLIAM and the EARL OF LEICESTER
are on horseback.*

19 – Leicester with Horse

WILLIAM:
AHORSE!
AHORSE!
AHORSE!

EARL OF LEICESTER:
YOUR GLORY WAITS!

WILLIAM:
AHORSE!
AHORSE!
AHORSE!

EARL OF LEICESTER:
SO DO NOT CRY!

WILLIAM:
AHORSE!
AHORSE!
AHORSE!

EARL OF LEICESTER:
NOTHING CAN BREAK YOUR FAMILY TIE!

WILLIAM:
AHORSE!
AHORSE!
AHORSE!

EARL OF LEICESTER:
AHORSE!
AHORSE!
AHORSE!

Scene 15

Morning at the Shakespeares'.

MARY:
The roosters have crowed!

20 – The Roosters (3)

THE ROOSTERS:
AAAAAHHH AAAAAHHH

MARGARET enters the kitchen. It's obvious that she hasn't slept a wink.

MARY:
Good morning, my girl. I need to talk to you.

MARGARET:
No time, Mamma my Mamma. I must run to the barn to fetch the eggs so I can cook them so I can—

MARY:
Shut. Up.

Long silence.

MARGARET:
Well, that was... interesting.

MARY:
Your brother has run off to London to join the theatre. To be perfectly frank, I thought he'd never stop clinging to his mother's skirts. You know, that young man has a serious— Are you familiar with the Oedipus complex?

MARGARET:
You must be proud, Mamma. Your son is becoming WILLIAM SHAKESPEARE. That's really something. Theatre. London. All that. What should I wash now?

MARY:
Stop playing dumb, you little dummy.

MARGARET:
Excuse me?

MARY:
William told me.

MARGARET:
Told you what?

MARY:
I'm proud of you. And I will never say that again. What were you thinking? You could have been killed. My baby. My daughter. My most precious love story. My child. Your brother promised me he'd keep your secret. But I need you to promise me you'll never write again: not even the tiniest little—

MARGARET:
Not a chance, Mamma.

MARY:
...

MARGARET:
If you say nothing. And William says nothing. Then I'm safe.

MARY:
All right: Go.

MARGARET:
...

MARY:
Take your father's horse and go to London. Go and watch that play that was born inside this head of yours.

MARGARET:
What?

MARY:
Do as I say. I'll make up something for your father.

MARGARET:
But Mamma—

MARY:
Hush, before I change my mind.

MARGARET:
Thank you.

MARY:
What's it like?

MARGARET:
What?

MARY:
How does it feel? All of... all that: reading, writing?

21 – *Wonderful*

MARGARET:
MAMMA, IT'S WONDERFUL
I WISH WE COULD SHARE IT
MAMMA, IT'S POWERFUL
TO LAUGH 'TIL YOU CAN'T BEAR IT
MAMMA, AND DID YOU KNOW
THAT THE WORLD'S BIG AND WIDE
MAMMA, MY SWEET MAMMA
THE LIGHT IS DANCING OUTSIDE

MARY:
MARGARET, HOW I WISH
TO SEE THINGS THROUGH YOUR EYES
MARGARET, TELL ME HOW
TO LAUGH UNTIL YOU CRY
MARGARET, TEACH ME NOW
THAT THE WORLD'S BIG AND WIDE
MARGARET, SHOW ME NOW
THE LIGHT THAT'S DANCING OUTSIDE

Scene 16

Dawn is breaking over London. THE EARL OF LEICESTER and WILLIAM arrive on the doorstep of the Globe Theatre. The sunrise is magnificent.

EARL OF LEICESTER:
Billy my Billy, how are you doing?

WILLIAM:
I don't know.

EARL OF LEICESTER:
How can you not know how you're doing when the only one who knows how they're doing is the one who's doing it?

WILLIAM:
I don't know.

EARL OF LEICESTER:
I find you morose. Look! London! Your new life! Here you shall be heard, seen, and celebrated.

WILLIAM:
What if I didn't write a single one of these lines?

EARL OF LEICESTER:
Is not your name on the title page?

WILLIAM:
Yes.

EARL OF LEICESTER:
Do I actually see tears in your eyes? Is that a skirt peeking out from beneath your breeches?

WILLIAM:
And what if a woman did create these characters? What's so funny about that?

22 – *Women and Girls*

EARL OF LEICESTER:
WOMEN AND GIRLS, WILLIAM
ARE MEANT TO WATCH THE WORLD GO
BY.
NOT LOOK AT IT AND THINK.

WOMEN'S GIFTS ARE IN THEIR LOOKS: IN
BEAUTY, NOT IN BRAINS.
A GENIUS CARES ABOUT HIS HEAD:
GIRLS, ABOUT THEIR HAIR.
FOR THEIR TINY MINDS ARE JUST AN
ITSY-BITSY SMALL AFFAIR.

WOMEN AND GIRLS, WILLIAM,
ARE MEANT TO WATCH THE WORLD GO
BY.
NOT LOOK AT IT AND THINK.

EARL OF LEICESTER:
Besides, their little hands get tired holding a pen. Anyway,
why were you asking me such a question?

WILLIAM:
Just because.

EARL OF LEICESTER:
That's what I find so moving about artists. They question
everything and nothing. Feeling better now?

WILLIAM:
Yes.

EARL OF LEICESTER:
Good, because we need to get straight to work. The cast is
waiting inside.

WILLIAM:
The cast?

EARL OF LEICESTER:
Of course, William. Surely you didn't think we'd be acting all the parts ourselves? You shall play Benedicta. Since, in 1577, women are not allowed onstage, all the female roles are played by men. We have to get ready: The Queen is coming on opening night.

WILLIAM:
The Queen?

Scene 17

23 – *Margaret with Horse*

MARGARET:
AHORSE!
AHORSE!
AHORSE!

FLEE INTO THE NIGHT

AHORSE!
AHORSE!
AHORSE!

HOPE MY ROAD IS RIGHT

AHORSE!
AHORSE!
AHORSE!

THERE'S LONDON IN THE LIGHT

AHORSE!
AHORSE!
AHORSE!

MARGARET:
And here's the theatre.

Scene 18

> *London. The Globe Theatre. In the wings. William can hear the crowd waiting. Suddenly, silence.*

WILLIAM:
  Why the sudden silence?

EARL OF LEICESTER:
  That's the ecstasy of a crowd on seeing the Queen enter the theatre.

WILLIAM:
  I can't do this. I can hardly breathe. I'm dizzy. I can't. I'm no good. Can't.

EARL OF LEICESTER:
  I watched you rehearse today. You have unbelievable talent. You are a superb actor. Now, get out there and show this crowd what a William Shakespeare can harvest from the depths of his guts. Whether the seed was planted by his own writing, or not.

Scene 19

MARGARET:

Go on, Margaret. Go in. You can do it. You know the word "Enter." But what if it was awful? What if they boo? They'll rip my innards out. Wait a minute: no one knows who you are! Get in there, Margaret. Can't do it. Can too. Can't. Can too. Can't. Can too.

> *She enters the Globe Theatre as if plunging into a cold lake. Before her, the stage. Refulgent light. During the final speech of her own play, she whispers all the words right along with the breathtaking performance of her brother.*

BENEDICTA (WILLIAM):

My love,
Never could I see thee shed one bead
Of blood, without I seek who did thee harm
And set my life at nothing till revenge.
And now thy blood is poured upon the ground,
A rich libation from an empty cup,
Which with my salt tears I would fain fill up.
Thou fad'st before mine eyes and in mine arms,
And all the harms that sore injustice gives
To all that lives, as well as he that dies,
If I could put them on and make thee free,
I'd do it in a trice, and cry, "Take me!"
Instead, my grief I wear upon my brow,
More proud than monarch of his gem-starred crown,
For Benedicta Gilborne is my name,
And with my words I'll long preserve our fame.
Lo! Now I speak our tale for all to hear,
And now they see the shape of all our wrongs,
This slanted world for shame doth hide its head.
So may our hands and souls forevermore
Be joined, defying all the apathy
And active malice of our petty tribe.
I come, my angel love, my prince, mine own:
May roses build cathedrals round our bones.

> *Benedicta dies. Applause.*

Scene 20

> *A dressing room. WILLIAM is alone, weeping.*
> *MARGARET enters, softly.*

MARGARET:
Want some cake?

WILLIAM:
Margaret!

MARGARET:
You were so… The most "so" I've ever seen in my life.

WILLIAM:
What are you doing here?!

MARGARET:
I needed to hear it. And you.

WILLIAM:
Seeing you. I'm.

MARGARET:
You're getting your costume all soggy.

WILLIAM:
I'm so ashamed. I feel like a coward and I—

> *WILLIAM stops. In the doorway stands the Queen*
> *(ELIZABETH I). Long silence.*

ELIZABETH I:
Shakespeare?

WILLIAM and MARGARET:
…

ELIZABETH I:
The words I heard tonight were. Were. Were. Indescribable.

WILLIAM:
(*Whispering to MARGARET.*) Am I dreaming, and a moment
from now I'll suddenly have no teeth?

MARGARET:
(*Whispering to WILLIAM.*) No, William. She's here. Right in front of us.

ELIZABETH I:
The rules are what they are. The laws were written by those gentlemen out there, but certain loopholes allowed me to find myself at the head of this nation. Their errors brought me to the throne. Just as their errors inflamed your rage. I felt it. I recognized it. It's the truth. Isn't it... my girl?

> *ELIZABETH comes over to MARGARET and takes her face between her hands.*

MARGARET:
You're going to have me killed, is that it?

ELIZABETH I:
You seem in rather a hurry to die.

MARGARET:
I think nothing of death if life forbids me to write.

ELIZABETH I:
In taking a husband, I would lose all my power... therefore, I have never known the joys of love.

24 – Searching

ELIZABETH I:
BEEN SEARCHING FOR SO LONG
SEARCHING
AND SEARCHING
'CAUSE I WON'T JUST PLAY THE PART
THEN YOUR WORDS, DARLING GIRL,
THEY CAME AND FILLED MY HEART

THEATRE, AND STORIES TOO
THEY LET ME MAKE BELIEVE
ABOVE ALL
THEY GIVE ME TIME AND SPACE

THE FREEDOM TO INVENT A MUCH
BETTER PLACE

A QUEEN MUST WEAR HER CROWN
ALONE
THERE'S PROTESTANTS AND CATHOLICS
AND PROBLEMS I COULD NEVER FIX
NO ROOM FOR CHILDHOOD DREAMS
NO FRIEND TO CALL MY OWN

(*Spoken.*) Actually, I always wanted to be a dancer.

BEEN SEARCHING FOR SO LONG
SEARCHING
AND SEARCHING
'CAUSE I WON'T JUST PLAY THE PART
THEN YOUR WORDS, DARLING GIRL,
THEY CAME AND FILLED MY HEART

ELIZABETH I:
Tonight, I experienced something like true love for the first time. I shall not have you killed.

MARGARET:
And of what use will life be to me?

ELIZABETH I:
You'll write, my girl: you'll write. And this marvellous boy—what a great actor you are—shall continue to wear the mask of the author. The witch-hunters shall leave you in peace, and you can continue to turn my heart inside out.

MARGARET:
You know that's impossible. Soon I must take a husband. Give him children. Raise them. Even if William agrees to stay silent to the end of his days—You know very well that I shall soon have no more "leisure" to devote to writing.

ELIZABETH I:
You shall live in my palace, never again to be burdened with domestic toil. I shall provide for all your needs.

WILLIAM:
(*To MARGARET.*) Are you going to say yes?

MARGARET:
...

WILLIAM:
Are you going to leave Mamma? And Papa? And have no children? Are you going to do all that? Are you?

MARGARET:
What about you?

WILLIAM:
...

MARGARET:
Would you consent to be William Shakespeare? Would you consent to take your place in History while leaving me a tiny little spot in your shadow?

ELIZABETH I:
If your sister accepts my proposal, I shall protect you as well.

WILLIAM AND MARGARET:
We'll think about it.

Scene 21

> *Night. In the Shakespeares' yard. MARGARET is looking at the stars. WILLIAM arrives, too happy to hide it.*

MARGARET:
You know what, William? I think these stars really are little fairies watching over us.

WILLIAM:
(*Too cheerful.*) ...

MARGARET:
Is that surprise on your face, or are you feeling unwell?

WILLIAM:
I love her so much we kissed I think I'm going to explode! She said my letter made her realize how she missed me. When she saw me, she cried: "William! William! You came back from London, I thought about it, I love you too, let's join the parade of love!" Then she kissed me. Like this:

> *WILLIAM starts kissing the empty air.*

MARGARET:
Ugh! No! Stop! I do not need to see that!

WILLIAM:
Have you made up your mind?

MARGARET:
I'm not sure. You?

WILLIAM:
Yes. If it's the only way you get to achieve your dream, then I say yes. And, fine: I admit I also love trampling the boards.

MARGARET:
It's called "*treading* the boards."

WILLIAM:
But I will respect your decision.

MARGARET:
So, if I go, you'll come with me?

WILLIAM:
Yes.

MARGARET:
And Amuletta? What will you do about Amuletta?

WILLIAM:
I don't know. I don't want to make her my handmaid in the
kingdom of Elizabeth I.

MARGARET:
I'm going to write, William.

And all of it, all, will be well.
All will be well.
All will be.
Well.

Isn't that right, little fairies?

> *The stars shine a little more brightly... and disappear*
> *into the night.*

25 – Epilogue

NARRATOR:
> And they lived happily ever after... or, unhappily 'til old age
> She behind the scenes, he upon the stage
> Oh how we all do love a happy ending
> Standing ovation, elation, curtain descending...

> Let truth be spoken: if Margaret had existed and resisted
> She'd have been beaten, broken, then burned
> Stone unturned, fate unearned

> And if by spectacular chance of miraculous circumstance
> she'd signed her name to those immaculate verses
> They'd've driven her words away in little hearses
> No icebreaker smashing and crashing a path for her
> No blossoming awesome iambics, amassing reputation and mystery
> Just toss 'em in the trash can
> The ashcan of History

> Do some women deserve to be immortal, pass through fame's portal, elevated with those genius men we've consecrated?
> Evidence and common sense say yes
> Your history books say no
> You feel progress is a line? Sometimes it's a pendulum, or a wheel
> In a hundred years, what girl will have her name
> Her glory
> Still be part of the human story?

> You? You? Maybe you?

> Margarets are sitting right here
> May they make their marks
> Monarchs of their own lives
> Their work survive the death-march of time
> Let none erase their glory from the heights

Their stories defaced would be a crime
But why must our sisters work alone for their own rights
As long as we brothers can still work our own mics?
Preach, say it strong, clear as a church bell
It's midnight and all is NOT well
Cuz we recognize "It's a Boy!" "It's a Girl!"
Still dictates the road we take, the shape and size of our world
No, no, no
Let's put *happy ever after* in our lives, not in a play
Let's say *once upon a time* starts here, with me and you
Today

The End.

Educator Resources

Quotes to Consider

"Universal History, the history of what man has accomplished in this world, is at bottom the History of the Great Men who have worked here."
– Scottish philosopher Thomas Carlyle, known for developing the "Great Man" theory

"For girls, you have to see it to be it. We stand on the shoulders of other women who have come before us."
– American composer Jeanine Tesori, from her Tony Award acceptance speech: she and Lisa Kron were the first all-female team to win Best Score, for *Fun Home*

"So while I can challenge Shakespeare, in truth, he's really a part of me. I'm part of this culture. It's part of the foundation of my own mythology, so me challenging Shakespeare is me challenging God, in terms of literature, because it's something that exists inside of me."
– Canadian playwright Djanet Sears, author of *Harlem Duet* and *The Adventures of a Black Girl in Search of God*

The following material is adapted from the study guide for the Stratford Festival production of *I Am William*.

Grade and Curriculum Connections

- Grades 3+
- Global Competencies: Collaboration, Communication, Critical Thinking, Creativity, Learning to Learn / Self-Awareness
- The Arts
- English
- Language
- Health and Physical Education
- Canadian and World Studies
- Social Sciences and Humanities

Synopsis

Margaret Shakespeare has a dazzling talent for writing, which she yearns to put to serious use. But in an age lethally suspicious of female intellect and literacy, how can she find a way to fulfill her authorial ambitions yet still survive? Fortunately, she has a brother, William, who isn't much of a writer but who wants to make it as an actor—and friends in high places have just the role for him.

Tapping into our fascination with the enigma of William Shakespeare's life and how he came to write those plays—and the seemingly endless speculation in some quarters about whether he really did—this lighthearted yet genuinely passionate interweaving of comedy, song and poetic fancy spins a playful and witty yarn that will delight younger audiences and adults alike.

Themes and Motifs

- Power and Freedom
  - Gender Inequity
  - Self-Determination
  - Identity

- Collaboration and Change
  - Allyship
  - Family and Sibling Relationships
  - Subverting Inequitable Systems

- Love of Language
  - Writing
  - Performance
  - Poetry

Discussion Questions

What's the relationship between history and truth?

Who decides what goes down in history?

Is there a historical moment, cultural event or personal experience that you think should be rewritten to tell a different story? What compels you to rewrite this story? What creative form would this rewrite take? (Now go and write it!)

What enables people to follow their dreams?

What does gender equity look like? What does it mean to you?

What are the qualities of a good sibling?

Why do people choose to write stories?

What are the reasons people write plays?

What surprised you most about the play?

Margaret loves writing more than anything and can't imagine her life without it. What in your life makes you feel this way?

Margaret and William's father, John, treats his two children very differently because of gender. Why do you think he believes this is right? What might prompt him to change his views?

The play is set at a time when Elizabeth I was Queen. How might having a female monarch have impacted the characters' attitudes toward women?

In what ways does William demonstrate allyship in the play?

What does Mary learn from her daughter, Margaret?

Exercise

Objective:
This exercise invites students to consider some of the key themes explored in the play: gender equity, writers/writing and history/fame.

Materials:
Library and/or internet access

Directions:
- Set a timer for three minutes and invite students to brainstorm and record as a class all of the writers that they know.
- Notice how many of these writers are men. If there is a big gender imbalance, ask students to talk about why they think this might be the case.
- Next, invite students in pairs or small groups to research a writer of their choosing who writes under a pseudonym. Ask them to share a little bit about their writing and the reasons why they chose to conceal their identity.

Debriefing Questions:
- What were the common themes across all of your chosen writers?
- How many of these writers are contemporary and how many of them are historical writers?
- What are the reasons why writers choose to conceal their true identities? How does gender impact this decision?

Online Resources

Shakespeare's Life, Folger Shakespeare Library:
https://www.folger.edu/shakespeares-life

Elizabethan Women in the Theatre, *The Atlantic magazine*:
https://www.theatlantic.com/entertainment/archive/2019/06/shakespeares-female-contemporaries/590392

The following material is adapted from the study guide for the Théâtre Le Clou production of *I Am William*. *(Guide written by Martin Lebrun in collaboration with Théâtre Le Clou.)*

Bio: William Shakespeare

William Shakespeare was born in 1564 in Stratford-upon-Avon, England, where he spent his youth. In 1577, at the age of 13, he left school to help his father, who struggled financially. Apart from these few facts, we know nothing about the teenage years of one of the greatest writers of all time.

We know that he was married at the age of 18 and that he had twins. Then between the ages of 21 and 28, he disappears completely from historic view. He reappears in London in 1592, where he is registered as an actor and playwright.

Shakespeare stands out as one of the most important writers of his time. During his lifetime he wrote some 37 plays and eight collections of poems.

He died in 1616 at the age of 52 in Stratford-upon-Avon and left behind a literary heritage often referred to as "universal."

Context

I Am William playwright Rébecca Déraspe imagines what could have happened during the period of Shakespeare's young life that historians know little about. What events pushed young William to embrace the profession of writer?

To reconstruct Shakespeare's youth, Déraspe uses the social context that reigned in England during the 16th century, both to fill in the gaps in the writer's biography and to echo our current social realities.

True or False?

How much do you know about gender equity in the world William Shakespeare lived in? Answer "True" or "False" to the following questions:

- In the 16th century, many women became doctors and lawyers.
  - ° False. Until the late 19th century, women in England were excluded from the university system and could not work in those professions.

- In Shakespeare's time, men played the women's roles onstage.
  - ° True. It was forbidden for women to perform in the theatre. (The movie *Shakespeare in Love* uses this fact as a plot device.)

- Queen Elizabeth I never married.
  - ° True. If she had married, her husband would have been given the power to rule England.

- During Shakespeare's time, both men and women wore poisonous face makeup.
  - ° True! White face makeup called "ceruse" was very popular in Elizabethan England, but because it was made of lead, it was poisonous and could be fatal. The alternative was to use pig lard that had been dried in the sun.

- Shakespeare's comedy *Twelfth Night* involves playing with gender roles.
  - ° True. In *Twelfth Night*, Viola sometimes dresses as a man and both a male and a female character have fallen in love with her. In the original production, the female roles were played by male actors. That means that the actor playing Viola was a man playing a woman playing a man!

Historical Fiction/Alternative History

Historical fiction involves a story that is set in a real place during a culturally recognizable time. The details and the action in the story can be a mix of actual events and ones from the author's imagination. Alternative history is a kind of historical fiction in which one or more historical events occur but are resolved differently than they were in real life.

A question haunted the playwright during the writing of the different versions of *I Am William*: "Do I have the right to change the ending? Do I have the right to say that Shakespeare is not who we believe him to be?" Using the idea that young William would have served as a figurehead for his twin sister, Rébecca Déraspe wrote this "alternative" version of history.

Exercise:
Choose a historical figure who was born before 1900 from the list below. Find a short biography of the person online and familiarize yourself with their accomplishments. How did gender play a role in their careers? Spend 15–20 minutes writing a story or play about an imaginary event that happened to that historical figure when they were your age, perhaps something that set them on their career path.

- Boudicca (Unknown–61 CE)
- Murasaki Shikibu (c. 976–c. 1026)
- Joan of Arc (1412–1431)
- Thanadelthur (1697–1717)
- Chevalier D'Eon (1728–1810)
- Olympe de Gouges (1748–1793)
- Marie Curie (1867–1934)
- Mary Ann Shadd Cary (1823–1893)
- Harry T. Buford (1842–1923)
- Emily Carr (1871–1945)
- Thérèse Casgrain (1896–1981)
- Amelia Earhart (1897–1937)